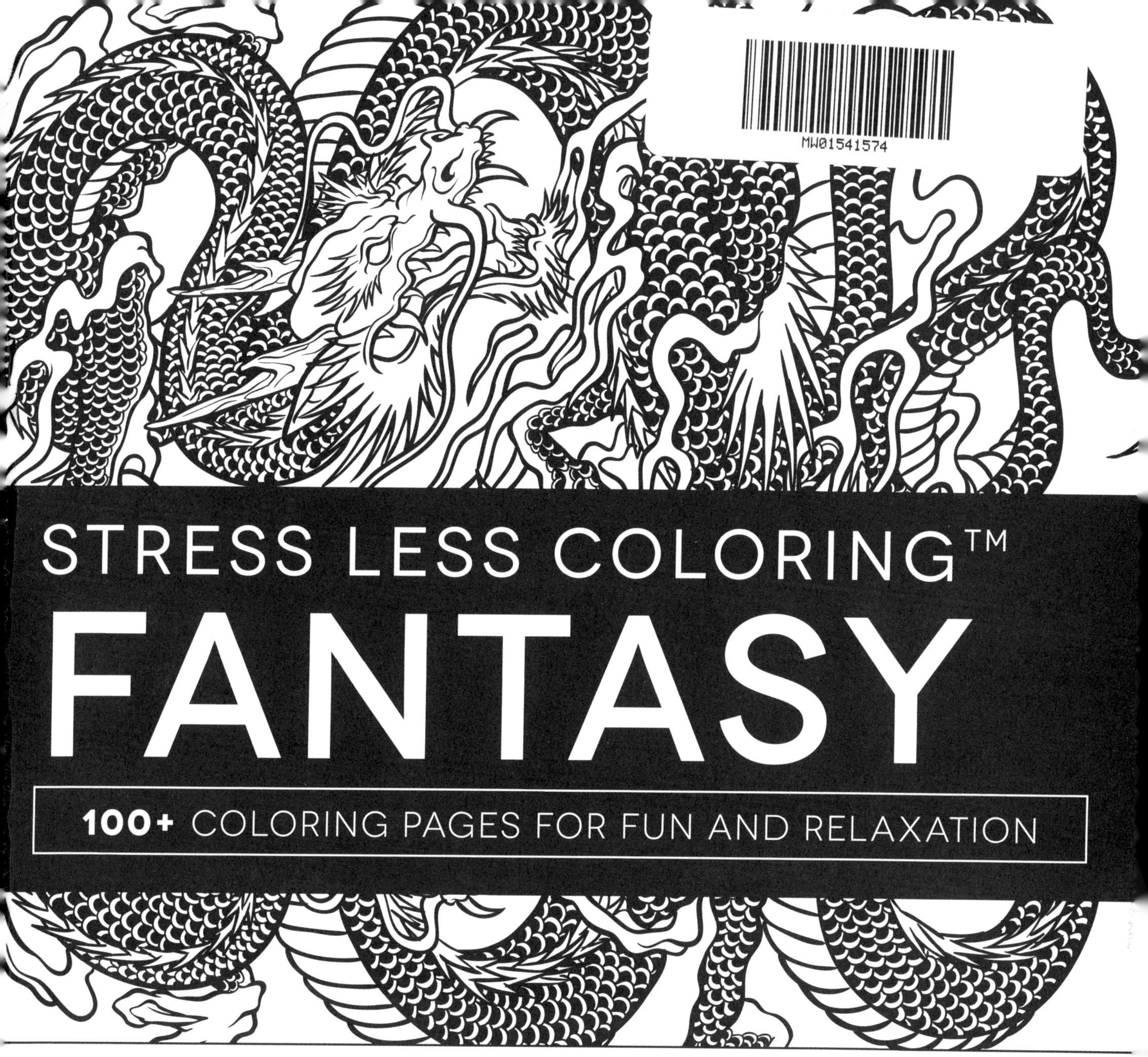

STRESS LESS COLORING™
FANTASY

100+ COLORING PAGES FOR FUN AND RELAXATION

Avon, Massachusetts

Copyright © 2016 by F+W Media, Inc.
All rights reserved.
This book, or parts thereof, may not be reproduced in any form without permission from the publisher; exceptions are made for brief excerpts used in published reviews.

Published by
Adams Media, a division of F+W Media, Inc.
57 Littlefield Street, Avon, MA 02322. U.S.A.
www.adamsmedia.com

Contains material adapted from *The Everything® Stress Management Book* by Eve Adamson, copyright © 2002 by F+W Media, Inc., ISBN 10: 1-58062-578-9, ISBN 13: 978-1-58062-578-4.

ISBN 10: 1-4405-9591-7
ISBN 13: 978-1-4405-9591-2

Printed in the United States of America.

10 9 8 7 6 5 4 3 2 1

This book is intended as general information only, and should not be used to diagnose or treat any health condition. In light of the complex, individual, and specific nature of health problems, this book is not intended to replace professional medical advice. The ideas, procedures, and suggestions in this book are intended to supplement, not replace, the advice of a trained medical professional. Consult your physician before adopting any of the suggestions in this book, as well as about any condition that may require diagnosis or medical attention. The author and publisher disclaim any liability arising directly or indirectly from the use of this book.

Many of the designations used by manufacturers and sellers to distinguish their products are claimed as trademarks. Where those designations appear in this book and F+W Media, Inc. was aware of a trademark claim, the designations have been printed with initial capital letters.

Cover design by Alexandra Artiano.
Cover images © iStockphoto.com/Tairy; iStockphoto.com/Natality.

This book is available at quantity discounts for bulk purchases.
For information, please call 1-800-289-0963.

INTRODUCTION

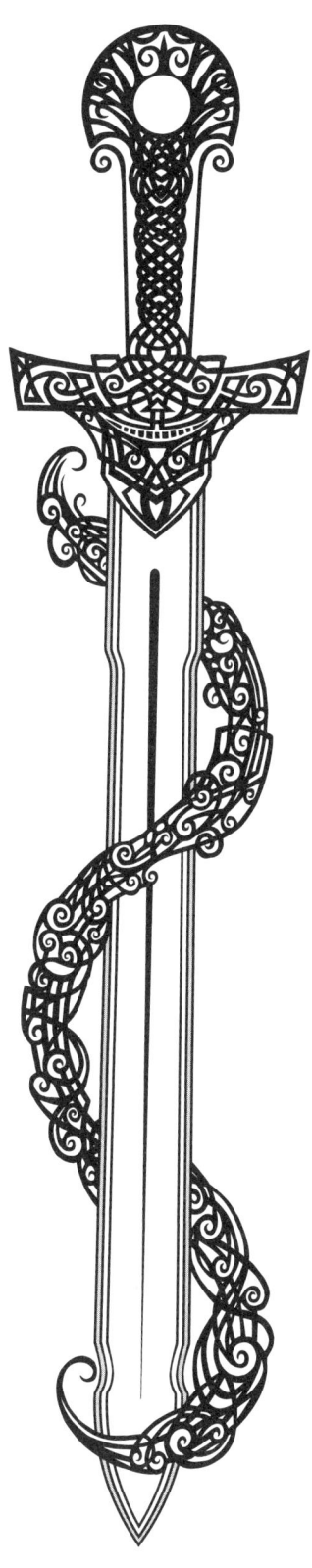

Looking to relax? Want to feel more creative? Need more peace and quiet in your life?

If you're looking to get rid of all the extra stress in your life, just pick up a pencil, crayon, or marker and let *Stress Less Coloring*™ *Fantasy* help you manage your worries in a fun, easy, and therapeutic way.

Over the years, studies have shown that coloring allows your mind to concentrate solely on the task at hand, which brings you into a restful state similar to what you can achieve through meditation. When you allow yourself to focus on the creative artwork in front of you, your mind doesn't have room for all the anxiety and stress in your life. And when your mind relaxes, your body follows, by letting go of any tension and giving you a sense of peace and well-being.

Throughout the book, you'll find more than 100 black-and-white prints depicting a variety of beautiful fantasy designs that are just waiting to be colored in. And the beauty of these prints is that you can color them in however you'd like. The most relaxing colors are cool shades such as greens, blues, and purples, but if you'd rather splash bold, bright hues like red, yellow, or orange across the page, feel free! Let your own unique palette guide your hand and personalize your pattern.

So whether you're new to art therapy or have been embracing the fun of coloring for years, it's time to stress less and find your inner calm and creativity—one fantasy print at a time.

Image © Olha Sukharevska/123RF

Image © Gennady Poddubny/123RF

Image © iStockphoto.com/SongSpeckels

Image © iStockphoto.com/Thoth_Adan

Image © iStockphoto.com/LuVo

Image © iStockphoto.com/i_panki

Image © Sorapich Pongsapan/123RF

Image © lian2011/123RF

Image © iStockphoto.com/Trudy Karl

Image © Olha Sukharevska/123RF

Image © rocich/123RF

Image © Alessandro Casazza/123RF

Image © iStockphoto.com/insima

Image © iStockphoto.com/quantum_orange

Image © iStockphoto.com/itskatjas

Image © Gennady Poddubny/123RF

Image © insima/123RF

Image © Gennady Poddubny/123RF

Image © iStockphoto.com/ElenaLux

Image © Shutterstock/masan4ik

Image © daicokuebisu/123RF

Image © iStockphoto.com/i_panki

Image © Shutterstock/masan4ik

Image © Giuliano Coman/123RF

Image © Tanantachai Sirival/123RF

Image © iStockphoto.com/itskatjas

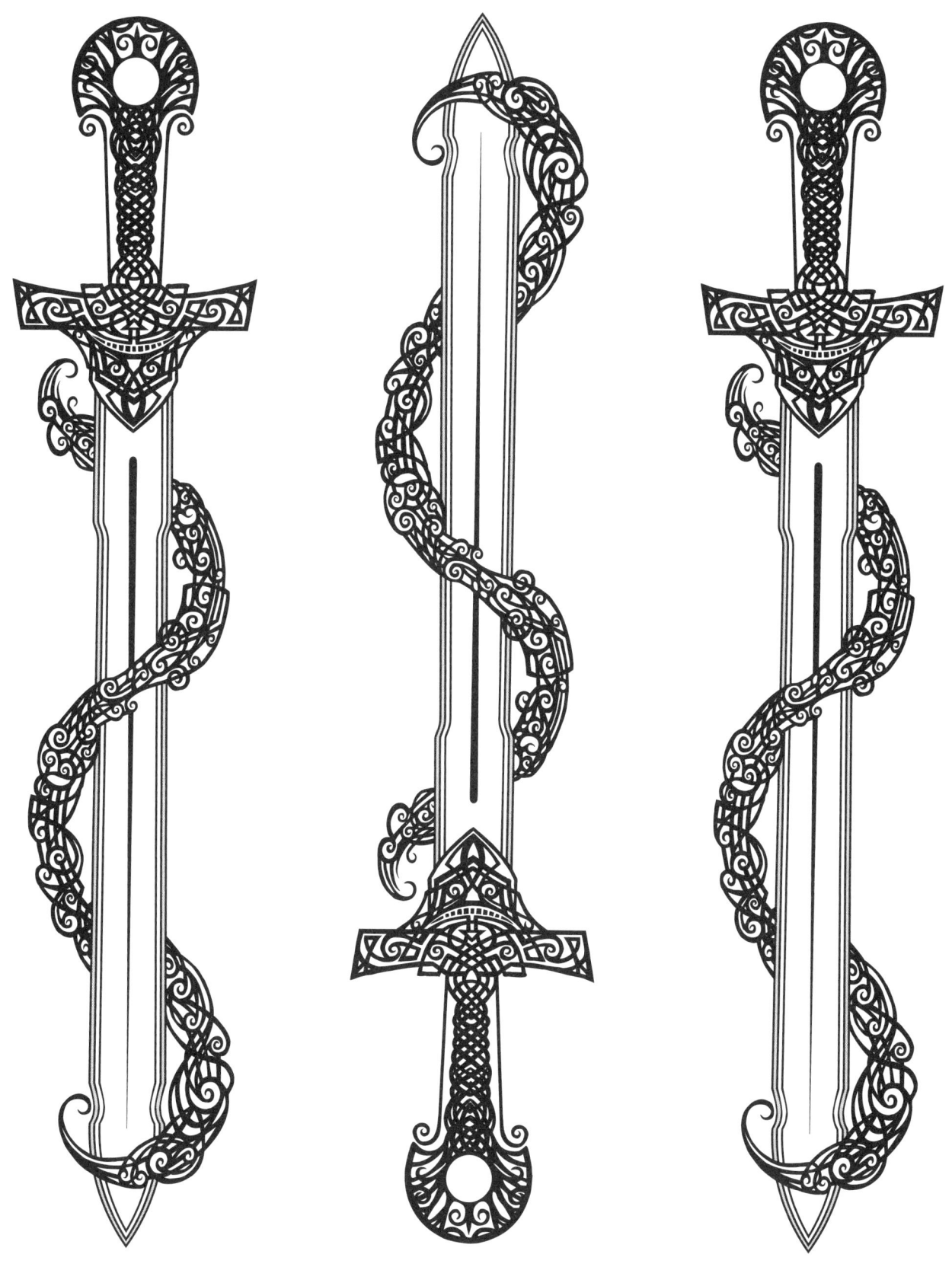

Image © iStockphoto.com/AlexeyBakhtiozin

Image © iStockphoto.com/NadiiaZ

Image © iStockphoto.com/Adelevin

Image © insima/123RF

Image © Aleksey Abramkin/123RF

Image © Olha Sukharevska/123RF

Image © seamartini/123RF

Image © Christos Georghiou/123RF

Image © bokasana/123RF

Image © iStockphoto.com/Trudy Karl

Image © Elena Matveeva/123RF

Image © Daria Troitska/123RF

Image © macrovector/123RF

Image © Irina Iarovaia/123RF

Image © bimdeedee/123RF

Image © Nadezhda Molkentin/123RF

Image © Olena Fedotova/123RF

Image © Ekaterina Nikolaenko/123RF

Image © mashabr/123RF

Image © seamartini/123RF

Image © bokasana/123RF

Image © Anna Pindyurina/123RF

Image © iStockphoto.com/doomko

Image © bimdeedee/123RF

Image © Gennady Poddubny/123RF

Marin, for love of Florimell,
In languor wastes his life;
The Nymph, his mother getteth her
And gives to him for wife.

Image © Ekaterina Nikolaenko/123RF

Image © iStockphoto.com/AlexeyBakhtiozin

Image © Gennady Poddubny/123RF

Image © iStockphoto.com/katritch

A teme of Dolphins raunged in aray
Drew the smooth chareit of sad Cymoent:
They were all taught by Triton to obey
To the long raynes at her commandement:

III · IV · XXXII

Image © 2009 Dover Publications, Inc.

Image © iStockphoto.com/AlexeyBakhtiozin

Image © iStockphoto.com/Garret48

Image © iStockphoto.com/AlexeyBakhtiozin

Image © iStockphoto.com/Tairy

Image © iStockphoto.com/CurlyBeard

Image © iStockphoto.com/AlexeyBakhtiozin

Image © iStockphoto.com/daikokuebisu

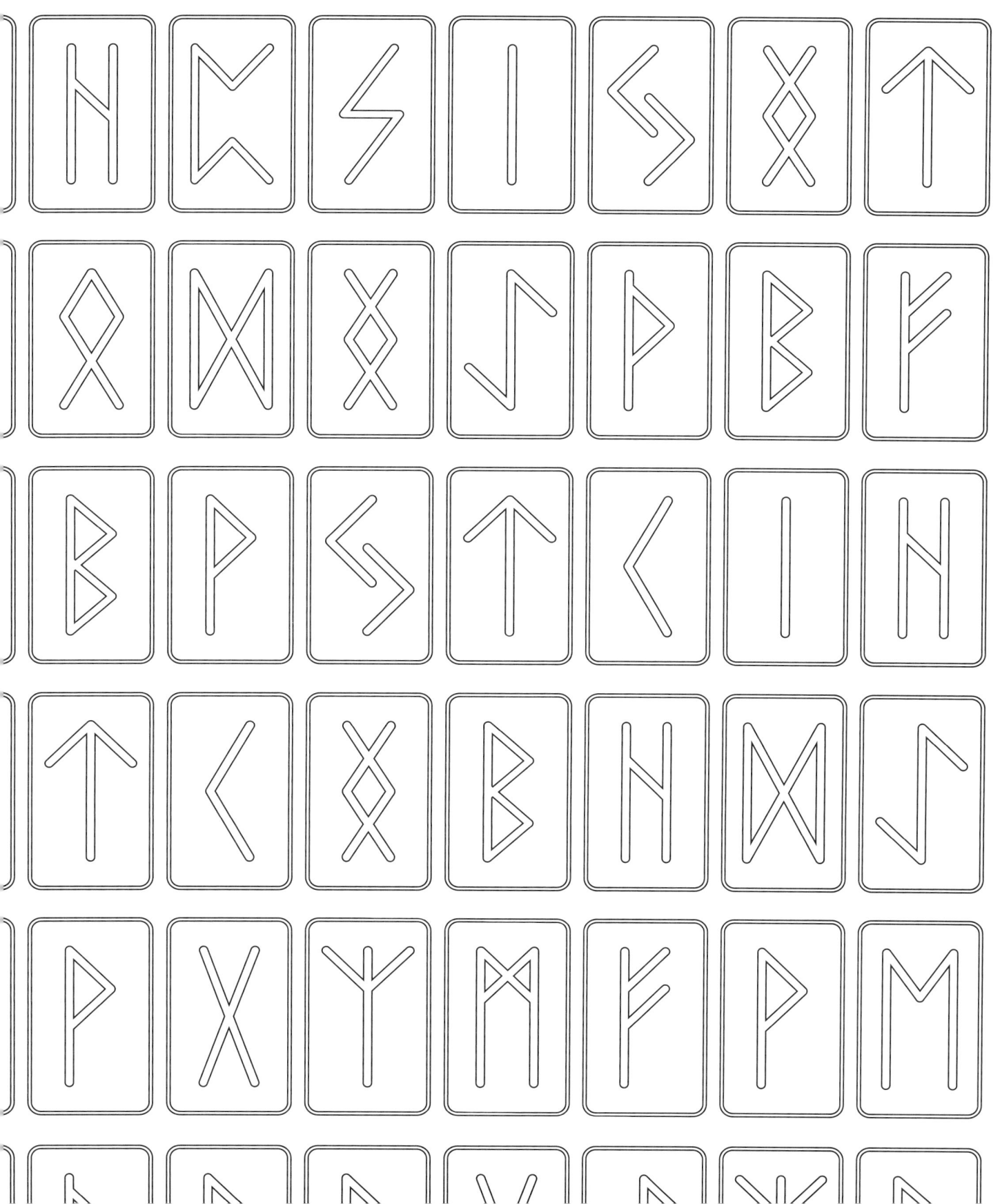

Image © iStockphoto.com/lilipom

Image © iStockphoto.com/stereohype

Image © iStockphoto.com/sanyal

Image © iStockphoto.com/itskatjas

Image © iStockphoto.com/Thoth_Adan

Image © Gennady Poddubny/123RF

Image © iStockphoto.com/AlexeyBakhtiozin

Image © drekhann/123RF

Image © Denis Barbulat/123RF

Image © rocich/123RF

Image © iStockphoto.com/MalyshFalko

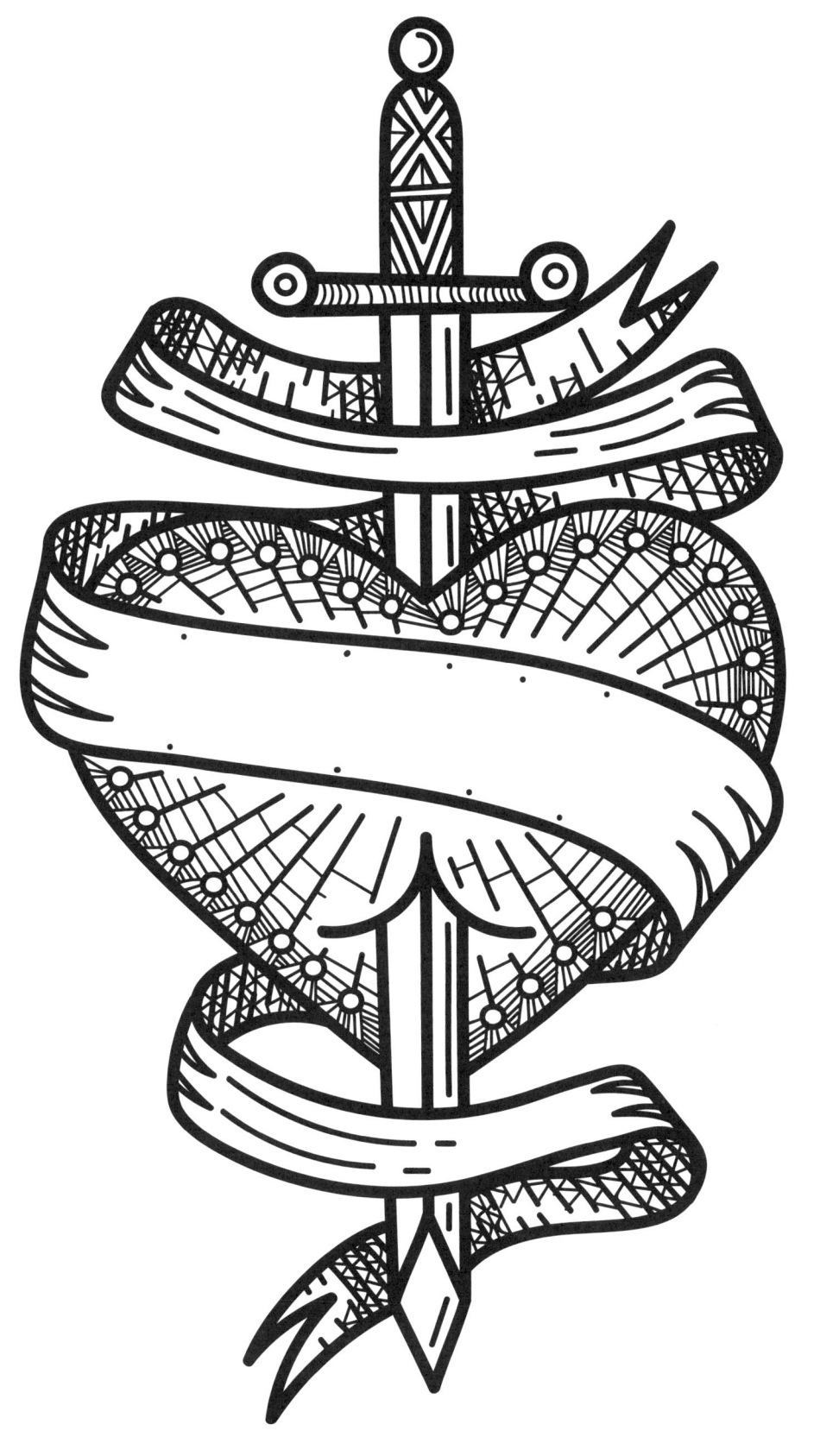

Image © iStockphoto.com/tinbee

Image © iStockphoto.com/Tazzina

Image © iStockphoto.com/vizualbyte

Image © iStockphoto.com/Kuo Chun Hung

Image © iStockphoto.com/quantum_orange

Image © iStockphoto.com/green216

Image © iStockphoto.com/katyau

Image © iStockphoto.com/VeraPetruk

Image © iStockphoto.com/Jobalou

Image © iStockphoto.com/pvg

Image © iStockphoto.com/Kuo Chun Hung

Image © iStockphoto.com/insima

Image © iStockphoto.com/itskatjas

Image © Weerayut Kongsombut/123RF

Image © iStockphoto.com/cidepix

Image © iStockphoto.com/daveturton

Image © iStockphoto.com/laluzm

Image © iStockphoto.com/Tairy

Image © iStockphoto.com/azat1976

Image © iStockphoto.com/seamartini

Image © iStockphoto.com/duncan1890

Image © rocich/123RF